SEVEN
THINGS
THAT HEAVEN AND
HELL HAVE IN COMMON

SEVEN THINGS

THAT HEAVEN AND HELL HAVE IN COMMON

JENNIFER WYNN

ARPress
ILLUMINATING IDEAS
EMPOWERING VOICES

ARPress
45 Dan Road Suite 5
Canton MA 02021
www.authorreputationpress.com
Hotline: 1(888) 821-0229
Fax: 1(508) 545-7580

Ordering Information:
Quantity sales. Special discounts are available on quantity purchases by corporations, associations, and others. For details, contact the publisher at the address above.

Printed in the United States of America.

ISBN13:   Paperback   979-8-89330-993-5
               eBook   979-8-89330-994-2

Library of Congress Control Number: 2024902479

Dedication

To YOU. May you find the path that leads towards The Light. And when you find that path, may you take it. And when you take that path, may you plant your feet firmly on it. And when you plant your feet firmly on that path, may you stand, may Peace befriend you and may you know Life as He is truly meant to be known. May you fly high, soar low and be filled with joy unspeakable. May you be kept safe. May you never know terror. May your future be brighter than the stars.

Acknowledgements

I wish to thank my beloved daughters, Abigail and Hannah, my pride and joy! I am honored to call you mine. And I am looking forward to an eternity in Heaven with you. I love you.

INTRODUCTION

Do you ever think about Heaven? What about Hell? What exactly are Heaven and Hell anyway? *Webster's New World Dictionary* defines Heaven as

1. the visible sky; firmament
2. a) the dwelling place of God and his angels, where the blessed go after death
    b) God
3. any place or state of great happiness

Hell is defined as

1. the place to which sinners and unbelievers go to eternal punishment after death
2. any place or state of misery, cruelty, etc.

Even though the dictionary does not capitalize those two words, I do, when I refer to them as locations. They are very real places. Towns, cities, even prisons are capitalized. So, I believe Heaven and Hell should be too. If something were to happen to you today, where would you go? Where will your loved ones go? Do you ever talk about it? Do you ever think about it? Or are you one of millions of people who lives for the here and now not for the there and then. Death scares you. Or you simply believe that once you're gone, you're gone. It's over. Done. Kaput. Or maybe you believe you're going to Heaven. Maybe you believe everyone is. You haven't killed anyone. You're basically a good person. You go out of your way to show people you care. So, you believe Heaven is in your future. I hope you're right. But you may not be.

Whatever frame of mind you have concerning the afterlife, I'm here like a voice crying out, "Heaven and Hell are real, and they have SEVEN things in common!" Let's get serious about the subject and allow our minds to stop with the busyness and focus for a minute. We are all heading to one place or the other. What is your destination? Perhaps once you read this book, you will change the direction you are heading. If that direction takes you towards The Light, then "Well done!"

Paths

What is a path? I'm sure you can make a fairly good guess. *Webster's New World Dictionary* defines a path as

1. a way worn by footsteps
2. a walk for the use of people on foot
3. a line of movement
4. a course of conduct, thought, etc.

Paths. There is a path to Heaven and a path to Hell. It's that simple. In fact, you are on one of those paths this very second, even if you're completely unaware of it. You're standing on it, walking on it, living, eating and breathing on it. And it's taking you somewhere you may not want to go. The path that leads to Hell is wide. It's broad and it's been traveled down by far too many people. Unfortunately, many humans don't know they're on that path until it's too late. Or maybe they do know and think they'll change paths someday. But death often comes calling at times when we least expect it and once it does there's no going back. No going back. No going back.

There is a path to Heaven, but it is narrow, and few find it. It's not hard to find. It's just that people don't look for it. They don't know it exists or maybe they do. But finding it and staying on it isn't important to them. This world is important to them. What they can see with their physical eyes, hear with their physical ears and touch with their physical hands. That's what matters to them. And money matters. Oh, how money matters! Possessions matter. Pleasures matter. But spiritual pursuits? That never occurs to them. They're too busy living for the moment. Their spiritual eyes are blind, their spiritual ears are deaf, and their spiritual hands are empty of any treasures that won't be burned up once they die.

Perhaps the very thought of paths that lead only one of two ways is repulsive to you. "Paths? Who needs paths?" you say. You have your own path. You do things your own way. You don't like following in other people's footsteps. You want to lead not follow. You're a natural born trail blazer. Blazing new paths is what you do. You don't want to go the way others have gone.

Well, you may like doing things your own way. But you have absolutely no power to create any other spiritual paths than the ones already in existence. You may behave differently than others who have gone before you on those paths, but you cannot change the paths themselves. And you certainly can't change where they lead to.

Which path are you standing on? Is it wide or is it narrow?

Gates

At the end of each path there are gates. Have you ever thought about that? Gates. Pretty cool, hah? *Webster's* defines a gate as

1. a moveable structure controlling passage through an opening in a fence or wall
2. a gateway
3. a movable barrier

*T*ry to imagine what the gates of Hell look like. CREEPY! Like the gates in front of the most horrifying haunted house you've ever seen on TV times a thousand. Or more. "Do you know where the gates of death are located? Have you seen the gates of utter gloom?" (Job 38:17 NLT). Gates of death and utter gloom, hah? Sounds ominous. Just how high and how dark and how thick are those gates? And where are they located? Are they made of iron, steel or some other kind of metal? How many gates are there? Who's standing watch? What kinds of creatures welcome you there, at the place where that path ends and the nightmares to surpass all nightmares begin? I don't want to know. What about you? I have no desire to see those gates in person or be greeted by any gatekeepers there. I think I'll pass. No, I definitely don't want to experience any of that firsthand. Remember, once you do there's no going back. No going back. No going back.

Let's move on to Heaven's gates. Now imagine a pearl. The most exquisite pearl you've ever seen. A polished pearl so pure and so clear that it's almost transparent. Perfectly round. Not a single flaw. An organic gem of such magnificence and rare quality that some would pay a fortune for it! So then, let's imagine that pearl on a much grander scale. A scale so grand that an enormous gate is made up of a single pearl. To the right and to the left of the gate are great and high walls. There are twelve pearly gates in Heaven and each gate is guarded by a holy angel.

In order to walk through the pearly gates, you must first enter through Jesus. He says, "I am the gate; whoever enters through me will be saved" (John 10:9 NIV). So, Jesus is the primary gate, and the pearly gates are secondary. You must pass through the First Gate to enter through the pearly ones. The test is simple. So simple that the majority of people don't pass because they can't fathom it could be that easy. So, they come up with all kinds of other ways to enter, but they come up short. Believe in Jesus. Believe that He is who He says He is. That's it. No strings attached. No catch twenty-two. No tricks. Just believe. Period. That'll get you through. Then the gates of Hell cannot prevail against you.

"Believe in the Lord Jesus, and you will be saved."

(Acts 16:31 NIV)

Souls

Souls. A lovely word. *Webster's* defines a soul as

1. an entity without material reality, regarded as the spiritual part of a person
2. the moral or emotional nature of man
3. spiritual or emotional warmth, force, etc.
4. vital or essential part, quality, etc.
5. a person
6. a feeling by U.S. blacks of racial pride and solidarity

The soul is the spiritual part of a human being. It does not die. Ever. Souls are eternal. Franklin Graham wisely said, "We'll never bury the real you. One day you're going to die; one day they're going to put your body in the ground. But your soul will live for eternity. Either it's going to be in heaven in the presence of God, or it's going to be separated from God in hell."

Souls. What could be more important? I can guarantee that NOTHING is more important to God. Absolutely nothing. Souls. Jesus said, "If any of you wants to be my follower, you must give up your own way, take up your cross, and follow me. If you try to hang on to your life, you will lose it. But if you give up your life for my sake, you will save it. And what do you benefit if you gain the whole world but lose your own soul? Is anything worth more than your soul? For the Son of Man will come with his angels in the glory of his Father and will judge all people according to their deeds" (Mathew 16:24-27 NLT).

Souls. How important are they to you? How important is your own soul to you? Souls are priceless to God. Yours included. He does not want you to go to Hell. Did you hear me? He takes no pleasure in watching anyone walk down that path. Please listen up! He created Hell for the wicked. He created Hell for Satan and the fallen angels, not for you. He wants you on the path that leads towards The Light, not on the path that leads towards deepest darkness, where the wicked will be buried in the dust and imprisoned in the world of the dead (Job 40:13 NLT). He wants your soul heading for those pearly gates of paradise. Period. There are no gray areas. It's black and white. God wants your soul and the souls of everyone you know and love to go to Heaven. But He will not make you choose that path. He is a gentleman. Yes. God is the perfect gentleman. Unlike many people you may know, He does not force a person to do something against his/her will. He gives you a choice and does His best to help you make the right one. But He respects you enough to allow you to make your own decisions and He painfully watches when you choose the most popular path. Just like a loving devoted parent who diligently trains his children how to behave in hopes they will make good and sound decisions when they mature, God hopes for you to make good and sound decisions too. This is particularly true of your choice to accept Wisdom regarding eternal matters.

What if you argue: "I didn't have loving parents! Mine were awful. I come from a divorced home. No love. No rules. I couldn't do a thing right. I was abused. What about that? Surely, God won't hold me accountable for not believing in Him. It's not logical. Where was He when I was going through hell? What was He up to then? How can He damn me for not being able to believe He actually cares? You know what? I don't think I even care where I end up. I don't want to have anything to do with a god like that. If there even is a god. A god who is absent. A god who watches the innocent suffer and starve. A god who brings calamities and allows pandemics that cause untold devastation in their wake. A god who refuses to put an end to violence and allows the violent to corrupt, pollute and abuse. If Heaven is where God lives, then I'll take my chances in Hell." To which I reply, "Whoa. Hold on there." If you can identify with any of those excuses or mindsets, I get it. I really do. And if you can, please hit the breaks and just breathe. God is not cruel. He is not out to get you. He does not damn anyone. Jesus died for all. People damn themselves. God's had His eye on you from the very beginning. HE LOVES YOU. Give Him a chance. He has your best interests at heart even if every single fiber of your being is begging to differ. Look at your pet. Look outside. Look at a tree or a flower or an insect. Those things came from the heart of God. God does NOT delight in evil. He rejoices in the truth. He is good, through and through. He may not have rescued you. I know what that's like, not to be rescued. I know what it's like to suffer. I've tasted indescribable pain and have had more than my fair share of heartaches, loss, trauma, tragedy and abuse. God allowed it. I will not pretend to have all the answers for the many why's and why not's. But I will tell you that God desperately longs for you to choose the high road. It may be a more strenuous climb. It may be the road less traveled. It may take all the strength and determination you have to stay on it. But it's the one He wants you on.

Heaven and Hell are filled with living souls. These souls have names. These souls have faces. These souls have birthdays. These souls may have the day that they physically died engraved on their tombstones, but that date is not the end of their existence. These souls have no second chance. No third chance. No fourth chance. No more chances.

Heaven and Hell. Souls are being added to their numbers daily. Even now, as you read, living souls are discovering Hell's gates or walking through pearly ones. It's not meant to scare you. It's meant to motivate and inform you. If you saw disaster coming and people you care about standing in the way of it, you'd do all you could to get them to safety. It makes perfect sense. I want you to be safe.

Five Senses

The five senses. Can you name them?

Seeing
Hearing
Touching
Tasting
Smelling

When a person dies, he does not lose his five senses. Souls have five senses too. Let's consider the first of the senses: seeing. Upon death, your spirit goes to one of two places. Your spirit looks just like you. You are fully able to see where you are heading. There are no blind spots. You know what's coming, like it or not. Take the path to Hell for instance. Chances are, you will be greeted by a gatekeeper and then dragged through Hell's gates to be tortured. You will have the ability to see the gatekeeper and the gates. You won't have the ability to avoid them though. So, let's consider the second of the five senses as it pertains to "The Hell Experience." Imagine a world filled with terrorized souls screaming to get out. Screaming. Souls can talk. They can scream too. But their screams don't accomplish a thing. They are screaming in vain. Yet you can hear it and soon you begin to scream too. Before long you realize you have a new body. One fit for destruction.

Let's change gears and compare Heaven to Disneyland. After all, Disneyland is nicknamed the Happiest Place on Earth. Heaven is the Happiest Place in Existence. People come from all over the planet to visit Disneyland. They save up their hard-earned dollars and often plan their trips to Disneyland months, if not years, in advance. They want to "experience the magic." At Disneyland, eye candy is everywhere. There is so much eye candy that you simply can't absorb it all in just one day. If you're in southern California, you can see Disneyland from the 5 Freeway. Seeing it from a distance is exciting! Once you've paid the entry fee you head for the entrance. At the entrance, you see a magnificent world awaiting you filled with laughter, music, singing, games, rides, satisfying treats and people smiling from ear to ear. Happy people. And you see Disney characters of all shapes and sizes come alive before your very eyes. It's where dreams come true.

Heaven is divine. It's beyond anything our minds are capable of imagining. It's Disneyland to the infinite power. You can see in Heaven. You can hear in Heaven. Like Disneyland, you want to take as many loved ones with you so they can have the time of their lives too. Only the fun never ends. You never have to leave, nor would you want to. Heaven is the ultimate Happy Place. No doubt about it. It's anything but boring. It's a constant feast for the eyes. And if you've been blind on earth, your vision will be restored to perfection. Same with hearing. If you're deaf, you'll be able to hear on a level unlike any earthly human can once you pass through those pearly gates. In fact, you will receive an entirely new body for your soul to live in! It will be like the bionic man or bionic woman, except that you will have super strength, super vision, super reflexes and other forms of superpower abilities all rolled into one. Even your mind will be transformed so that you operate with high forms of intelligence. This is no joke. New bodies and super powers await you in Heaven. There is no suffering in your body there. No fear. No torment. No screaming. Just constant rejoicing over all the awesomeness!

The third of the senses is touching. You will have the ability to feel and to touch in both Heaven and Hell. In Heaven, you can hug your loved ones. You can stroke the animals. You can swim in the River of the Water of Life that's as clear as crystal and you can dance to the glorious beats all around you. No worries. No cares. No pain. No one can use or abuse you there. No evil is allowed. No violence. No manipulating. No conditional love. No ulterior motives. None of that sort of stuff is in Heaven. Unconditional love is the rule for everyone's conduct. No exceptions. And your new body and new mind enable you to meet that one basic requirement. It doesn't take effort. It comes naturally and flows freely. A gift from God.

Unfortunately, people still have the ability to touch and be touched in Hell. That's too bad. Like I've said, the first time a person realizes this will probably be when he or she is grabbed and pulled through those wicked gates. But the touching and the being touched does not end there. Hell is filled with creatures. Nasty ones. I'll cover that topic in the next chapter and that's a chapter I guarantee you won't want to miss.

The fourth of the five senses is tasting. Tasting. What exactly does it mean to taste? It means the sense by which flavor is perceived through the taste buds on the tongue *(Webster's)*. Food is important to God. So important, in fact, that the Bible promises that Jesus Himself will host a huge banquet for the saved in their honor. Not in His honor. IN THEIR HONOR. For choosing the high road/narrow path. But I want to clarify that the banquet is not for everyone who chooses the high road, but only for those on the high road who were prepared for His return. There is a difference. It is possible to be on the high road and not be prepared. What will be served? Hopefully, some really aged wine! Maybe that's wishful thinking on my part, but I can wish. I'm certain there will be no meat on the menu because there is no killing in Heaven. Other than that, it's anyone's guess. I know there is fruit in Heaven. The Tree of Life bears twelve crops each year, one for every month. And its leaves are edible too.

Food isn't in Hell. Drinks aren't either. Not even water. Souls are in a perpetual state of thirst. Their throats are dry, and they are thirsty 24/7. They are never able to quench their thirst. They aren't even allowed one drop of water. Not one drop. Remember Lazarus and the rich man? Lazarus was in Heaven, the rich man in Hell. The rich man was so parched that he couldn't get water off his mind so he asked if Lazarus could simply dip one of his fingers in water to cool the rich man's tongue for refreshment. Now the rich man had to be pretty desperate to ask for only a finger drop of water. He was probably trying to hedge his bets and concluded that his chances for having a request granted would be more favorable if he kept his request to the bare minimum.

But he was wrong. He was not allowed even a finger drop of water to provide relief. He was given nothing to quench his thirst, to moisten his lips, to cool his tongue. Absolutely nothing. So, food and water aren't in Hell, nor can food or water be taken there. Yet the desire to taste will not dissipate.

Smelling . . . the last on the list of the five senses. Just what does Hell smell like? Do you really want to know? Well, it smells. You had better believe it smells. And it doesn't smell good. It smells like burning sulfur. That is Hell's trademark. What is sulfur? Sulfur is a pale yellow, non-metallic chemical element: it burns with a blue flame and a stifling odor. Stifle means 1. to smother or suffocate 2. to suppress; hold back: stop. Stifling means to die or suffer from lack of air *(Webster's New World Dictionary).*

The sulfuric smell in Hell is so rancid and difficult to inhale that it produces suffocation. Only in Hell you can't die, so you continually suffocate. With an environment that smells like that, it's no wonder that Hell is a land of gloom and confusion, where even the light is as dark as midnight (Job 10:22 NLT). Unlike Heaven, where everyone has their wits about them, Hell creates confusion and disorder. Remember, once you find yourself its prisoner, there's no going back. No going back. No going back. And you know this. You know the torture will never end. There's no hope. There's no relief. There's no waking up from this nightmare because you already are awake. There's no rest for your soul in Hell. And then you remember. And the remembering is even more torturous than anything Hell could throw at you. You remember your mother's Bible that she kept next to her bed. You remember the guy on your football team who always wanted to pray before a game. You remember the way your buddy kept asking you to join him at church, and the way your grandma got that worried look on her face every time you told her that Christianity wasn't for you, but you didn't mind that she was so into it. You remember the way others belittled Christians and even though you weren't a Christian, it bothered you. And you remember (Oh and you WILL remember!) books like these and every other attempt that God made to point you Heavenward. You will even remember the simple joys of earth. The sounds of seagulls. The sounds of the ocean and waterfalls and rain. The sounds of voices from people you love. The sounds of a tranquil night. And this knowing, this remembering, this contemplating over all you've lost and never will have again because of the choice YOU made, because of the path YOU chose, will be the most wretched and painful and torturous thing of all. That YOU could have prevented it if you really wanted to. But it wasn't important enough to you to do it when you had the chance.

Reader, I don't want you to have to bear that load, to experience such regret and mental anguish. I don't care who you are or what you've done or haven't done. Jesus went through Hell so you wouldn't have to. There's not one soul that He didn't die to save. Not a single one. It makes no difference who you are. God Himself says, "I take no pleasure in the death of anyone. Repent and live!" (Ezekiel 18:32 NIV).

So, stop this very second and choose the right path, the path that leads towards The Light. Then Hell's smells won't ever enter your nostrils. Heavenly aroma awaits you once you do. And heavenly aroma is just that. Heavenly.

Living Creatures

*T*here are other worldly living creatures in both Heaven and Hell. They are either for you or they are against you. They are highly intellectual, vary in size, shape and form and have wills of their own. Like humans, they are eternal. Because they cannot die, they are also immortal. They have personalities. They also have different job descriptions, meaning that they specialize in certain fields and are the best at what they do in each field. Some have a supernatural ability to take on human form. Many of them are extremely active in our world but, for the most part, they are invisible to the human eye. They never sleep. And they are absolutely extraordinary!

Let's begin our study by identifying the living creatures in Heaven.

1. Seraphim: plural for seraph. *Webster's Dictionary* defines a seraph as a heavenly being or any of the highest order of angels. There are four seraphs. Each one is full of eyes, around and within, front and back. The first of these living creatures looks like a lion. The second like an ox. The third has the face of a man and the fourth looks like a flying eagle. Each of these four living creatures has six wings, also covered completely with eyes, inside and out, even under its wings. With two wings they cover their faces. With two they cover their feet. With two they fly. Seraphim are caretakers with spiritual powers. They surround and care for God's throne. They can talk. They are worshipers. "Day after day and night after night they keep on saying, "Holy, holy, holy is the Lord God, the Almighty—the one who always was, who is and who is still to come." (Revelation 4:8 NLT) Their voices sound like thunder. At the sound of their voices,

Heaven's doorposts and threshold shake. They also have the ability to purify. Wikipedia defines seraphim as a type of celestial or heavenly being of the highest rank in Christian angelology, who are literally "burning ones." In Hebrew, "Sarap" means "to burn." The word is sometimes used for venomous snakes (e.g., Isaiah 30:6), possibly due to the burning sensation of the poison. Many Biblical translations interpret this scripture as "fiery flying serpent." It is often used alongside, or interchangeably with "nachash," a common and generic term for serpents (e.g., Numbers 21:6-7). Serpents? In Heaven? Have you ever heard that before? My guess is you probably haven't. These are holy fiery creatures! Being that I have at times, day dreamed of taming my own fierce, frightening and fire breathing dragon and naming her Flame, I find these creatures particularly intriguing, lovely and desirable and would jump at the chance to go for a ride on one, if possible! Giddy up! I believe that the seraphim burn because of their fiery passion for God Almighty. Seraphim are also musicians. They sing and play the harp. I wholeheartedly believe that music is the language of angels. Seraphs are responsible for holding golden bowls filled with incense, which are the prayers of the saints. This incense fills God's nostrils with a pleasant fragrance. Kind of like the way a scented candle or burning incense works on our senses. Seraphim not only worship God with their instruments and voices, they worship God by falling down before Him in reverence as a demonstration of their love, adoration and respect.

2. Cherubim: plural for cherub. The dictionary defines a cherub as a winged angelic being in the second exalted order of the celestial hierarchy, who attends on God. A cherub is often falsely represented as a chubby, rosy cheeked child with wings, such as Cupid. So, I am here to tell you that a real live cherub looks nothing like a child! That myth was birthed in the Renaissance era and people have believed it ever since. Cherubim are splendid, awe-inspiring and downright magnificent creatures who appear like burning coals of fire! There are at least four cherubim. Perhaps even seven. These living creatures are beasts of the most holy kind. Beasts. They have the body/form of a

man yet they each have four faces. One face looks like a man, one like a lion, one like an eagle and one like an ox. The face of the ox is a cherub's true face. The face of an ox! Not of a child. Wikipedia says that the four faces represent the four domains of God's rule; the man represents humanity; the lion, wild animals; the ox, domestic animals; and the eagle, birds. I tend to disagree with this interpretation. Others say that the faces are a man representing love, a lion for justice, a bull for power and the eagle for farsighted wisdom and insight. This makes more sense to me. Cherubs have straight legs. They also have the feet of an ox. These feet/hooves gleam like burnished bronze. Each cherub has four wings and when in flight, these wings touch each other. They conjoin. Cherubim spread their wings to rise. With two wings they fly and with two they wrap/cover their bodies. Under these wings, on their four sides are the form of a man's hand. Cherubim are protectors. They are holy creatures. They surround themselves with an immense cloud, flashing lightning and brilliant light. Bright fire moves back and forth among them when they are in flight. Cherubim operate with such speed that their movements appear like flashes of lightning and their wings sound like rushing waters or like the tumult/uproar of an army. When these living creatures come to a halt and stand still, they lower their wings.

3. Ophanim: plural for ophan. Ophan means "wheels." Wikipedia defines an ophan as one of a class of celestial beings called ophanim. There are four of these living creatures. They are eye-covered wheels (each composed of two nesting wheels) that move next to the winged cherubim, beneath the throne of God. The Bible calls them "the whirling wheels." Their bodies are luminous and appear like fire. Their rims are high and awesome. They are giant living creatures who are literally the flaming wheels and carriers of God's holy throne. Wow! Ophanim are closely connected to the cherubim because the spirit of the cherubim is inside of them. When the cherubim move, so do the ophanim. When the cherubim stand still, the ophanim do too. When the cherubim rise, the ophanim rise. They are perfectly in sync. If the ophanim are the chariots of

God's throne, then the cherubim are God's charioteers. What does this mean? It means that the King of Kings and Lord of Lords has a throne. It is above and beyond the circle of the earth. This throne doesn't always stay in the same place, meaning that He travels! If you're in a pit, maybe He's coming to rescue YOU! If you're not on the right path, now would be a good time to jump on it! And if you hear the sounds of thunder and see an immense cloud with lightning flashing back and forth out of it, much more may be going on than meets the eye.

4. Erelim: plural for erel. There are twenty-four erelim/elders. The erelim sit on twenty-four thrones that surround God's throne. Wikipedia says that erilim are generally seen as the third highest rank of divine beings. Erilim means "valiant and courageous." These living creatures are clothed in white, have gold crowns on their heads and look like men. They are musicians who sing and play the harp. Like the seraphim, they too are carriers of the golden bowls of incense. When overcome with the wonder of God, they fall down in worship before the Almighty. When they fall, they lay their crowns before God's throne and join the seraphim in proclaiming the holiness of God.

These living creatures that I have mentioned are like God's senate and serve in His court. They are celestial beings in a class of their own. They love God incessantly and find their joy and purpose in unbroken fellowship with Him. They are extremely powerful, keen and insightful. The level of their intelligence cannot be measured. They bathe in God's presence and radiate a beauty incomprehensible to the human mind. They are virtuous. They love God passionately for who He is and are fiercely loyal to Him. They are His friends and closest companions. Some friends and companions! God sure has awesome buddies, wouldn't you say? O Happy Day... Any friend of His is a friend of mine. I'm on the narrow path, by the way.

5. Archangels. The dictionary defines an archangel as an angel of high rank. Archangels are warrior angels who fight spiritual battles. They are of the highest rank in the Lord's armies, of which the Lord Himself is Commander in Chief. These armies

also include horses and chariots of fire. Archangels are protectors who guard nations and countries. Michael is chief prince among the archangel princes. He is the mighty protector of Israel. If you have ever seen the Transformer movies, imagine that Michael is like Optimus Prime, only he can never die, because angels are immortal. Archangels are extremely skilled in warfare. They are armed and highly equipped with spiritual weapons. These living creatures are wholeheartedly devoted to God, are at His disposal and are His friends.

6. Angels. An angel is a messenger of God, an immortal spirit. The Bible makes no mention of them having wings. Not all angels are the same size, and they differ in rank and authority. Angels look like men, even in spirit form. There is no reference in the Bible that any angelic being looks like a woman. The seven angels of God's judgment are clothed in white, clean shining linen and wear gold sashes around their chests. There are four angels in the book of Revelation who are described as being so mighty that they each take a position on one of the four corners of the earth by standing with one foot on the land and one on the sea. From these positions they together can hold back the four winds of the earth to prevent any wind from blowing on the land or the sea or on any tree. Whoa! Those are some powerful and enormous angels. And those mighty angels take orders from a different angel who is higher up in rank. Yikes! There is another angel in the Book of Revelation who is described as being so remarkable and glorious that he is robed in a cloud, with a rainbow above his head. His face shines like the sun and his legs are like fiery pillars. He also has the ability to plant his left foot on the earth and his right in the sea and when he shouts, it's like the roar of a lion. We're not talking Jesus here, we're talking angel (Revelation 10). No wonder the apostle John fell at an angel's feet to worship him, but the angel told him, "Don't do it. I am a fellow servant with you… Worship God!" These aren't the typical angels one usually thinks about when one thinks of angels. I should say. Yet they exist and they are on God's good side. There is also an angel who operates with such a great level of authority and who radiates such splendor

that he can illuminate the entire earth. This living creature can light up the whole world! Which I find fascinating! Like the seraphim and erelim, some angels are musicians. Many angels play trumpets, not harps. There is also an angel who carries a golden censer and is tasked with offering incense to God on the golden altar in front of God's throne. The smoke of the incense and the prayers of the saints rise up before God from the angel's hand. One day this angel will hurl this censer to earth, and it will cause thunder, rumblings, flashes of lightning and an earthquake. That's some golden censer! There are thousands upon thousands, and ten thousand times ten thousand angels. They sing, praise and worship God. They rejoice in God's works and celebrate when a soul chooses the right path. They have the ability to take on human form, when necessary. They are instruments of God's judgments. They are God's servants who minister to humans in whatever way God chooses. They also serve as soldiers in God's armies to fight for human souls. They are good. They are obedient. And they have supernatural power and abilities. They are and will always remain loyal to God. And they would love nothing more than to see you on the right path, to give you a big high five and a tender pat on the back for choosing The Light, Jesus Christ, The Light of the World.

Now, let's identify the living creatures that will be in Hell. Some are there already. They are spirits who fell out of Heaven because God kicked them out for inciting a rebellion against Him.

1. Satan, often referred to as Lucifer, is the leader of this rat pack. He is also called "the devil" which means "chief evil spirit." Currently, he is free to roam to and fro across the earth. He and his followers specialize in murder, theft and destruction. But "the fallen," to borrow a fitting phrase from Transformers, will never rise again. They will never be granted the privileges they once enjoyed. They have no access to God's throne unless they are ordered or summoned there by God. Satan gave up a position of the highest honor to pursue his dream. What was his dream? He dreamed of being worshipped. He wanted more recognition. He desired to be served. He talked himself into

believing that being a servant was beneath him. So, he rebelled. He was so convincing that he single handedly deceived 1/3 of the angels. They bought into his deceitfulness and rebelled with him. Now, Satan wanted to outshine God, so to speak. He wanted the worship due to God alone. So, you really have to wonder just what this living creature must have been like to risk all he had going for him. Keep in mind that he really thought his dreams could come true, even though he was created, and God was his creator. He actually thought this was a possibility! If he was anything like some of the angels I've mentioned, it would be no wonder why he felt he was "big stuff." Humans let our egos get the better of us and we're only human. Even the archangel Michael wouldn't enter into a dispute with Satan after he fell, which leads me to conclude that Satan outranked Michael in Heaven and is still more powerful than Michael. The name Michael means "one who is like God." If Michael is like God, what must Satan have been like if he was even greater? It's certainly something to consider. Now, in the end time battle Michael and his angels do win against Satan and his demons, but there are two times more angels than demons, so demons have no shot at winning. It is interesting to note that the Bible says, "Satan and his demons," meaning that Satan is the highest ranking official of that demonic army or the demonic forces. So, in a way, he got half his wish. At least the demons serve him. I bet some of them have regrets about that. But there's no going back, not even for the fallen.

Lucifer means "shining one." Given everything we know about heavenly beings, this translation can be taken literally. In fact, the Bible calls seven angels "stars" in Revelation 1:20. Satan was as bright and brilliant as a star. You can see stars at night. I wonder if some of the stars we see are angels. Could be. I wonder if the star that led the wise men to Christ's manger was an angel. Did you know that even now, Satan has the ability to masquerade as an angel of light? As we have learned, cherubim also surround themselves with light. Hmmm. I wonder. Let's see… What else was Satan like before he decided he deserved to be worshipped? Ezekiel 28 paints a descriptive picture. Satan was the model of perfection, full of wisdom and perfect in beauty. Perfect. What a word. Every precious stone adorned him. He was the most beautiful heavenly creature God made. The Bible tells us that God created and anointed Satan as a mighty angelic guardian, a guardian cherub, who walked among the fiery stones and served directly at God's throne. So, Satan was a cherub... God's guardian and charioteer, until he decided to be wicked. Cherubim are mighty beasts, remember. How sad. To give all that up. For what? For Hell? Satan knew better. But let's not stop there. Revelation 12:9 NIV says, "The great dragon was hurled down—that ancient serpent called the devil, or Satan, who leads the whole world astray." What other living creatures are called serpents? Seraphim! So, Satan was also part seraph, in my opinion. But let's keep going. In Isaiah 14:13 and Revelation 2:13 we are told that Satan had a throne in Heaven and now has one on earth. What living creatures have thrones? Erilim! Could Satan have possibly been the absolute highest form of celestial being that God ever created? A combination of a seraph, a cherub and an erel all rolled into one? He was adorned with ruby, topaz, emerald, chrysolite, onyx, jasper, sapphire, turquoise and beryl jewels, which were all set in gold. Remember, he was perfect. There is no other celestial being described that way. I believe he was the only one of his kind and that it is possible that Satan was the most powerful, glorious and god-like creature God ever created. And if he was not the most powerful celestial creature, then he was one of the most powerful. Besides the qualities I've already mentioned, Satan is described in the King James Version as containing percussion instruments, e.g., tambourines, as well as stringed instruments such as flutes and harps (similar to the sounds of a synthesizer) within the confines of his very own body. The Septuagint or LXX does not seem to make this distinction in the Koine Greek version of the Hebrew Bible, but it is widely believed that Satan was, indeed, the angel of music and that he widely influences music to this day. Jewish tradition claims that Satan has twelve wings, as stated in Talmudic literature. That is very likely. And this living creature, this Satan, broke God's heart in a way no mere man could ever comprehend. God put tremendous thought, love and care into creating Satan and yet he chose to spit in God's face. If that wasn't disrespectful enough, he convinced a third of the angels to corrupt themselves by spitting in God's face too.

Satan deceived the holy angels and polluted them. Now they are forever banned from enjoying heavenly privileges and destined to live a life in darkness and regret. Make no mistake. Even angels who sin reap what they sow. It's a spiritual law. The Lake of Burning Sulfur is their final destination. What is yours? Has Satan deceived you? He'd love to take you with him; to cohabitate with you in Hell. Not because he's fond of you, but because he knows how much God loves you and how much God grieves when you choose the wrong path. And Satan loves to see God grieve. Believe me, God does grieve. Our wrong decisions and behavior fill His heart with pain. Satan gets his kicks off it. And the fact that humans are made in God's image only makes Satan hate us more! That's what motivates him... Hate and his sick and twisted sense of humor. He is determined to take as many human beings to Hell as possible. It's his obsession. He lives for it. Breathes for it. He never stops strategizing how to do it and won't rest because he's consumed with it. He'll stop at nothing to keep people on the wrong path or to cause them to fall off the right one. If that is possible. He is a deceiver, a tempter, an accuser. He is slanderous. Don't give in to him. You will pay the price if you do. By now, I hope you know better.

2. Territorial spirits. They are dark princes. Like archangels, they are spirits who rule over territories. They are extremely powerful, hostile and give their allegiance to Satan alone. They should not be messed with.

3. Familiar spirits. These are demons that familiarize themselves with people such as witches. They stay close by, like family. They "attach" themselves. Familiar spirits don't just hang around those involved in Satanism or witchcraft, though. Familiar spirits can familiarize themselves with people who don't fight them off. Fear is a common familiar spirit. Lust is too. So is depression. There are many types of familiar spirits, but that doesn't negate the fact

that the human heart can be afraid, lustful, depressed and so on and so forth without the presence of these spirits. For indeed it can and most often is! One should never justify human behavior by saying that he/she is being enticed by unseen forces or he/she just can't help himself/herself. I struggle with fear... Primarily the fear of abandonment. And I don't do lonely well. Do you? I cuss from time to time. It's true. What's more is that more often than not, I'm too darn hard on myself and that can make me depressed. I am a human being with real emotions and reactions to life. But I have learned over years of trial and error how to distinguish when I'm at war with my humanity and when I'm at war with evil. A thankful and forgiving heart and a focused life are great weapons against these emotions and powers. So are the weapons of purity, honesty, integrity, humility, optimism, obedience, prayer, faith, hope, love and the Word of God.

4. Ordinary demonic spirits. Without a doubt, demons thrive off being involved in human affairs and will stay involved as long as possible. They oppress, harass, annoy, manipulate and discourage. They are ordered to kill, steal and destroy and delight in ruining relationships. They are also associated with curses. They are nasty living creatures who come in different shapes and sizes. They vary in strength and in rank. I believe that some demons are even afraid of Satan. They are distorted and gruesome. They are dark. They are real. And they are probably trying to distract you from reading about them. Many of them seek refuge in a body, whether man or animal. They don't like being kicked out, so you should never take one on unless God tells you to. It will only make matters worse if you try it without God's permission. For the most part, these living creatures/demons are warriors, skilled in human defeat.

**I would like to stop here for a minute to say that the most powerful weapons against these evil forces are the Blood of Christ and the Word of God. Jesus came to set the captives free! No evil can stand against Him! And He is for YOU!

5. Nephalim: plural for Nephal. Although scripture does not make their origins perfectly clear, it is widely accepted and

believed that they were half-human half-demonic or fallen angel. There were many Nephalim before the great flood. As you can imagine, they were gigantic and had unparalleled strength. 1 Enoch claims that these giants were 450 feet tall. They are extinct. This topic leads a person to ask many questions, the primary one being: Did fallen angels procreate? The Bible says that "in those days, and for some time after, giant Nephilites lived on the earth, for whenever the sons of God had intercourse with women, they gave birth to children who became the heroes and famous warriors of ancient times" (Genesis 6:4 NLT). I believe the "sons of God" refer to fallen angels since the earth turned completely evil afterward and God had to wash it clean. According to Wikipedia, the word "nephal" is derived from the Hebrew root npl, meaning "to fall." Therefore, it is conceivable that God's primary purpose/goal for the flood was to rid the earth of the Nephalim. "And I remind you of the angels who did not stay within the limits of authority God gave them but left the place where they belonged. God has kept them securely chained in prisons of darkness, waiting for the great day of judgment" (Jude1:6 NLT). Maybe the angels who procreated are the ones who are now bound. Jude goes on to explain that Sodom and Gomorrah also gave themselves up to sexual immorality and perversions and were punished for it, implying that the angels were punished for sexually immoral behavior too. Many scholars would tell you that this is a play on words and that the Bible doesn't refer to angels procreating at all. The Bible does say that souls will be like the angels in Heaven and not procreate, so I see both sides. But note, it specifically references Heavenly angels, not demonic ones. The Bible also makes it clear that spirits can take on human form. Genesis 6:4 implies that the Nephalim inhabited the earth during not one, but at least two different time periods. Wikipedia states, "The footnotes of the Jerusalem Bible suggest that the Biblical author intended the Nephalim to be an "anecdote of a superhuman race." This Bible, the Dead Sea Scrolls and Aramaic Enochic literature all support the belief that a Nephal's paternity was that of an angel. Whoever the Nephalim's fathers were, there is no argument that giants did exist and that these beings had supernatural physical grandeur.

Many of the living creatures that I have mentioned have studied and mastered the science of human behavior. They can often predict how humans will respond in any given situation. Because they have history on their side, they are usually quite accurate. But angels and demons aren't the only living creatures in Heaven and Hell.

Animals. Yes. There are animals in Heaven. Thank God. I can't imagine living in a world without animals. Unfortunately, Hell is such a world. Let me tell you what the animal kingdom in Heaven is like.

The wolf will live with the lamb,

the leopard will lie down with the goat,

the calf and the lion and the yearling together;

and a little child will lead them.

The cow will feed with the bear,

their young will lie down together,

and the lion will eat straw like the ox.

The infant will play near the cobra's den,

and the young child will put its hand into the viper's nest.

They will neither harm nor destroy on all my holy mountain,

for the earth will be filled with the knowledge of the Lord

as the waters cover the sea.

Isaiah 11:6-9 NIV

If you've ever wondered if animals are in Heaven, you never have to wonder again.

Now Hell is a different story. According to Isaiah 14:11 NIV, there are only two types of living creatures in Hell besides demons. Worms and maggots. And I have a feeling they are much larger and more grotesque than the ones you find on planet earth. The fire can't kill them nor can you. They were specifically designed to torment. In fact, did you know that the giant tube worm, which currently dwells on the floor of the Pacific Ocean, can reach a length of seven feet ten inches and tolerate high hydrogen sulfide levels? Worms will torment souls in Hell. Gross! Makes you cringe.

If you haven't leaped onto the right path, just what are you waiting for? If you're scared, ask God for help. His Son was led like a lamb to the slaughter. Jesus Christ paid the price with His blood. Just believe it, receive it and thank God for it. Don't fight it. Just believe. Now's not the time to worry about what other people think. If tears need to come, then let them come. If anger needs to come, don't hold back. Let it out! Scream if you have to. Punch a wall if you have to. Say, "Trusting you is hard to do God! I have so many why's without answers, so many contradictions in my head. So many reasons for not letting go. But I hear You, I really do. I want to be on the right path. Please, help me." Asking God for help is a wise thing to do. In his distress, King David called to the Lord. He cried to God for help. God heard David's voice from His temple. David's cries came before God into His ears. And, according to Psalm 18 NIV, this is what happened next…

The earth trembled and quaked, and the foundations of the mountains shook; they trembled because God was angry. Smoke rose from his nostrils; consuming fire came from his mouth, burning coals blazed out of it. He parted the heavens and came down; dark clouds were under his feet. He mounted the cherubim and flew; he soared on the wings of the wind. He made darkness his covering, his canopy around him—the dark rain clouds of the sky. Out of the brightness of his presence clouds advanced, with hailstones and bolts of lightning. The Lord thundered from Heaven; the voice of the Most High resounded. He shot his arrows and scattered the enemy, with great bolts of lightning He routed them. The valleys of the sea were exposed, and the foundations of the earth laid bare at His rebuke, at the blast of breath from His nostrils. He reached down from on high and took hold of David and rescued him from his foes, who were too strong for him. Then God put David into a spacious and safe place.

God Does Answer Prayer!

The Element of Fire

*T*here before me was a throne in Heaven with someone sitting on it. And the one who sat there had the appearance of jasper and carnelian. A rainbow, resembling an emerald, encircled the throne. From the throne came flashes of lightning, rumblings and peals of thunder. Also, before the throne there was what looked like a sea of glass, clear as crystal.

There came a voice from above the expanse over the heads of the cherubim as they stood with lowered wings. Above the expanse over their heads was what looked like a throne of sapphire, and high above on the throne was a figure like that of a man. I saw that from what appeared to be his waist up he looked like glowing metal, as if full of fire, and that from there down he looked like fire; and brilliant light surrounded him. Like the appearance of a rainbow in the clouds on a rainy day, so was the radiance around him.

He was dressed in a robe reaching down to his feet and with a golden sash around his chest. The train of his robe filled the temple. His head and hair were white like wool, as white as snow, and his eyes were like blazing fire. His feet were like bronze glowing in a furnace, and his voice was like the sound of rushing waters. In his right hand he held seven stars, and out of his mouth came a double-edged sword. His face was like the sun shining in all its brilliance.

And God said, "I am a great king. A son honors his father and a servant his master. If I am a father, where is the honor due me? If I am a master, where is the respect due me? All day long my name is constantly blasphemed. Behold, I am coming soon. My reward is with me, and

I will give to everyone according to what he has done. I am the Alpha and the Omega, the First and the Last, the Beginning and the End. Yes, I am coming soon."

And at his feet was an altar filled with living and burning coals of fire (Revelation1, 4 & 22, Isaiah 6 & 52, Ezekiel 1 and Malachi 1).

Fire. What is it about fire? Seraphim are called "burning ones." Cherubim and ophanim look like they're on fire. Christ, in His glory, appears full of fire. Even His eyes blaze. In fact, God and God's tongue are both called "a consuming fire" in the Bible. God appeared as fire to Moses when He introduced Himself as "I AM THAT I AM." Abraham saw a smoking firepot with a blazing torch during one of his encounters with God. So, just what does fire have to do with it? In Heaven, fire represents purity. Ever heard of "the refiner's fire?" It's a term used to describe how fire has a refining or purifying effect. Have you been through refining fire? I have. I've spent the better part of my life in the fire. And when I thought it couldn't get any hotter, it did. What does the fire feel like? Well, let's just say it's hell. And it's about as close to Hell as I ever want to come.

In Hell, you are literally on fire. You can't escape. Ever. You're aware that there are happy people, free people, whole people out there. But you never get to know what that's like. The burning never ends. The flames never die. You can't crawl out. You can't escape. You can't alleviate your pain. You just can't. And my guess is you wish you'd never been born.

There is fire in both Heaven and Hell. And there are fire wardens/ guardians. A holy angel has fire duty in Heaven. Demonic creatures have fire duty in Hell. In Heaven, fire represents purity. In Hell, fire represents judgment. In Heaven, fire is a beautiful thing. In Hell, fire is a horrifying thing. In Heaven, fire is used to bless… As in the case of Isaiah when a seraph touched his lips with a fiery coal. In Hell, fire is used to punish. But in both Heaven and Hell, the fire never goes out. Flames burn perpetually, night and day, forever, without interruption. And the flames are extremely hot, even in Heaven. So hot, in fact, that a cherub, as mighty as it is, has to use tongs to touch the coals that burn in the fire. A cherub's powers are no match for the flames. If cherubim, or "the burning ones," can't touch the fire with their hands, that's saying a lot!

The element of fire. What a thing. I remember 9/11. Do you? I remember watching the horrors of it on TV. I remember seeing people jump out of windows to their death to escape the flames. I remember the terrified looks on their faces. Some of them were holding hands. Being killed by being crushed on the ground seemed like a better option than being burned alive. I remember. People were desperate for relief. I remember that it all seemed so surreal, like it wasn't possible, like it couldn't actually be as bad as it was. I remember the chaos, the confusion, the mayhem. I remember the firefighters. I remember their sacrifice. I remember the screaming, the desolation, and the looks of hopelessness on people's faces as the reality of 9/11 began to sink in. I remember the way that people were running and hiding and falling and frantically searching for shelter. They wanted to be safe. I remember tears. I remember sirens. I remember third degree burns. I remember the way so many people appeared lifeless, such emptiness and sadness in their eyes. Such brokenness. Eyes are the window to the soul. I remember. And I remember the love. Those who laid down their lives for people they never met. Those who worked tirelessly around the clock looking for survivors. Those who refused to lose hope. Those who were left picking up the pieces. And I remember how dreadful it was to watch as people discovered that their loved ones would never be coming home.

Fire. Don't let it threaten your future. I beg of you. Please don't.

Eternal Divide

*H*eaven and Hell have a boundary in common. It is a great divide or chasm that separates the two in order to prevent souls from crossing back and forth. It is permanent, everlasting and impossible to conquer.

CONCLUSION

Look down. You are standing on a path, and I am curious… What does it look like? For there is a path that seems right to a man but in the end, it leads to death. But the path of life leads upward for the wise to protect them from eternal doom. Who are the wise? Those who fear, honor and believe God and His Word. And all who call on the name of the Lord will be saved!
(Proverbs 15:24, 16:25 & Joel 2:32).

www.ingramcontent.com/pod-product-compliance
Lightning Source LLC
Chambersburg PA
CBHW060357130626
46553CB00003B/1276

* 9 7 9 8 8 9 3 3 0 9 9 3 5 *